EXPLORING OUR SENSES

Seeing

For a free color catalog describing Gareth Stevens' list of high-quality books, call 1-800-542-2595 (USA) or 1-800-461-9120 (Canada). Gareth Stevens' Fax: (414) 225-0377.

Library of Congress Cataloging-in-Publication Data

Pluckrose, Henry Arthur.
    Seeing/by Henry Pluckrose; photographs by Chris Fairclough.
        p. cm. -- (Exploring our senses)
    Includes bibliographical references and index.
    Summary: Photographs and text illustrate how we use our eyes to
drive, read, and see things big and small and far away or close up.
    ISBN 0-8368-1288-3
    1. Vision--Juvenile literature. [1. Vision. 2. Senses and sensation.]
I. Fairclough, Chris, ill. II. Title. III. Series.
QP475.7.P58   1995
612.8'4--dc20   94-23770

13284
9/00

North American edition first published in 1995 by
Gareth Stevens Publishing
1555 North RiverCenter Drive, Suite 201
Milwaukee, Wisconsin 53212, USA

This edition © 1995 by Gareth Stevens, Inc. Original edition published in 1985 by The Watts Publishing Group. © 1985 by Watts Books. Additional end matter © 1995 by Gareth Stevens, Inc.

Additional photographs: J. Allan Cash 8, 9, 24; by kind permission of The Guide Dogs for the Blind Association 30; Peter Millard 29; ZEFA 7, 10, 15.

Printed in the United States of America

1 2 3 4 5 6 7 8 9 99 98 97 96 95

Seeing

By Henry Pluckrose
Photographs by Chris Fairclough

Gareth Stevens Publishing
MILWAUKEE

Shut your eyes.
Keep them closed for a moment.

4

Without your
eyes, you are
unable to see.

Our eyes are like windows. They let us look out on the world.

6

Our eyes need light to see. During the day, light comes from the sun.

8

At night, artificial lights
help us see.

Our eyes can
see tiny things —
like the spots on
a ladybug . . .

**and huge things —
like an excavator.**

Our eyes can see
things nearby . . .

and things far away.
In the distance,
even big things
look small.

With just our
eyes, the moon
is a tiny ball in
the sky.

Through a telescope, the moon looks like this.

Our eyes help us
understand the world.
We can see whether
things are hard or soft,

and whether things are difficult or easy to reach.

The world is full of color.
Our eyes can see colors.

18

Which colors do you like best?
Which ones do you use for painting?

STANDARD WHITE
WEISS
BLANC STANDARD
BLANCO NORMAL

LEMON
ZITRONENGELB

BRILLIANT GREEN
BRILLANTGRÜN
VERT BRILLANT
VERDE BRILLANTE

AZUL BRILLANTE

TAN BLUE
CYANBLAU
BLEU CYAN
AZUL CIAN

CERISE
KIRSCHROT
CERISE
CEREZA

CRIMSON
KARMESIN
CARMIN
CARMESI

BRILLIANT RED
BRILLANTROT
ROUGE BRILLANT
ROJO BRILLANTE

JET BLACK
PECHSCHWAR
NOIR JAIS
NEGRO AZABACHE

Some colors are used to send messages. Red often means "Stop!"

Green often means "Go!"

21

Some people find it hard to
tell green from red.
Can you see a number here?

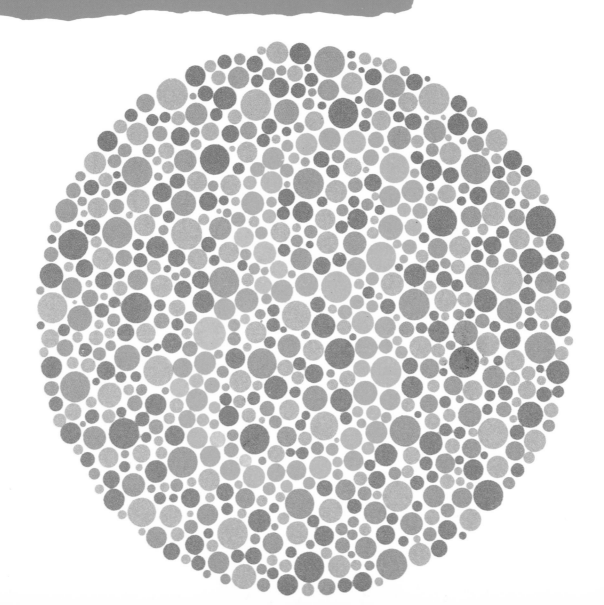

We never stop
using our eyes,
except when
we are asleep.
We use them
when playing . . .

23

when riding
a bike . . .

when watching a show . . .

25

or when looking at books.

Without sight,
no one could drive
a bus or a car . . .

27

or use giant
machines.

Not everyone has perfect sight. Some people need eyeglasses. Glasses help us see more clearly.

Some people cannot see at all. Trained dogs can help guide them.

Shut your eyes.
Keep them closed.
What can you see?
Open your eyes.
Look and see.

More Books to Read

Look at Your Eyes. Paul Showers (HarperCollins)
Look — What Do You See? Jennifer Rye (Troll)
Why Do Some People Wear Glasses? I. Asimov and C. Dierks (Gareth Stevens)

Videotape

You — And Your Eyes. (Disney)

Activities for Learning and Fun

1. Eye Spy You can play this game with a friend or family member. Place seven to ten small objects on a serving tray. Cover the tray with a towel, and take it off for one minute so the other player can study the pieces you have collected. Cover the tray again, and let the other player try to name all the pieces on the tray. Then, without letting the other person see, remove one object from the tray. Put the tray in front of the other player again. Can he or she guess what object you have removed?

2. Seek-and-See Some animals are difficult to spot in nature even when you are looking right at them. These animals have fur or other body coverings that blend in with their surroundings. This is called camouflage. A simple experiment can show how camouflage works. Count out twenty candies in different colored wrappings. Then outline a circle about 5 feet (1.5 meters) across with string outside on the grass. Scatter the candies inside the circle. Try to point out all twenty candies. Are some easier to find than others? Which were the hardest to see?

Index